12/94 World Almanac

D1412188

SEALS

SEALS

Annette Barkhausen and Franz Geiser

Gareth Stevens Publishing
MILWAUKEE

A N I M A L F A M I L I E S

For a free color catalog describing Gareth Stevens' list of high-quality books, call 1-800-341-3569 (USA) or 1-800-461-9120 (Canada).

The editor would like to extend special thanks to Shelley L. Ballmann, Oceans of Fun, Inc., Milwaukee, Wisconsin, for her kind and professional help with the information in this book.

Library of Congress Cataloging-in-Publication Data

Barkhausen, Annette.
   [Robben. English]
   Seals / Annette Barkhausen and Franz Geiser. — North American ed.
     p. cm. — (Animal families)
   Translation of: Robben.
   Includes bibliographical references and index.
   Summary: Briefly explains the evolution of the pinniped family and describes the physical characteristics, habitat, and behavior of various kinds of seals, sea lions, and walruses.
   ISBN 0-8368-0842-8
   1. Seals (Animals)—Juvenile literature. 2. Eared seals—Juvenile literature. 3. Walruses—Juvenile literature. [1. Pinnipeds. 2. Seals (Animals)] I. Geiser, Franz. II. Title. III. Series.
QL737.P64B37513 1992
599.74'5—dc20
                                                      92-10684

North American edition first published in 1992 by
Gareth Stevens Publishing
1555 North RiverCenter Drive, Suite 201
Milwaukee, Wisconsin 53212, USA

Series editor: Patricia Lantier-Sampon
Editor: Charles R. Bennett
Translated from the German by Sabine Beaupré
Editorial assistants: Diane Laska and Barbara Behm
Editorial consultant: Shelley L. Ballmann

Printed in MEXICO

2 3 4 5 6 7 8 9 98 97 96 95 94 93

Picture Credits
A.G.E.—2, 7 (middle right), 9 (lower), 29, 35; A. Barkhausen—7 (upper left); British Museum—7 (upper right); Circus Knie—10 (right); Bruce Coleman—Alexander 8-9: Bartlett 34: Blake 20: Dawson 13 (upper right): Erize 11 (walrus), 24, 26, 36: Everson 7 (lower): Foott 13 (lower), 14, 18 (lower), 30-31: Lanting 32: Lightfoot 21 (left): McCarthy 1: Reinhard cover, 12-13, 40; Hans D. Dossenbach—9 (upper right), 11 (Northern sea lion), 37, 38, 39; Franz Geiser—10 (left); Jacana—Balthis 30 (left): Ferrero 25, 28: Gohier 23, 27, 33: Lemoigne 21 (right): Soler 18 (upper): Varin 8 (left): Walker 4 (left); Motovun Archive—6; NHPA—Dickens 17: Hawkes 11 (Southern elephant seal): Johannes 4-5: Leach 11 (Common seal): Palo 4 (right); Reinhard-Animal photos—11 (Australian sea lion); Silvestris—Konig 16; WWF—11 (Monk seal), 22.

Table of Contents

What Is a Seal?

Below: *This drawing of a seal and sea lion was made during an expedition to Alaska in 1741.*

We have all seen playful seals on television or in books or at zoos. But scientists really do not know very much about seals. They swim in the water, but they aren't fish. They crawl on their stomachs, but they aren't snakes. They have names like sea lion, leopard seal, and elephant seal. But seals are not related to lions, leopards, or elephants.

Millions and millions of years ago, seals lived on land. Their ancestors were probably something like bears. Over the centuries, though, seals changed from land animals to sea animals. During this time, seals underwent many changes that helped them to live in the water. For one thing, their bodies slowly became streamlined so they could glide easily through the water. Another change was that their four limbs became shorter and their feet changed into flippers, which helped them swim. When sea lions, fur seals, and walruses swim, they use their front flippers as oars. Their rear flippers help their balance. "Earless," or "true," seals swim by moving their rear flippers.

Sea lions, fur seals, and walruses use all four flippers to walk on land, a process helped by a rotating hip bone. True, or earless, seals, however, have a harder time moving about; they are very clumsy and awkward on land. They use only their front flippers to move, and their bodies drag along the ground.

Some seals, such as the common seal and the monk seal, live in warmer water areas.

To help them survive in the cold, seals have heavy coats. But more important to keeping warm is the thick layer of fat seals have below their skin. This fat is called *blubber.* In a way, seals are built like thermos bottles. The layer of blubber wrapped around their insides keeps them warm. For example, seals can stay on ice for a long time, and the blubber keeps them insulated from the cold. The blubber also stores energy, which gives the seals nourishment at times when they do not eat and also helps them float in the water. Seals are mammals, and their body temperature is about the same as other mammals, 98.6° Fahrenheit (37° Celsius).

Cold Homes

Most seals live near the coastlines or ice of the North and South poles. Many seals also live in the cooler oceans and seas of the world.

Newborn Seals

Seal pups may be born on land or on ice. The hooded seal pup, for example, is born on an ice floe, a floating mass of ice. It weighs about

Below: The Anguit was a seal spirit that the Inuit of Kalaallit Nunaat (Greenland) worshipped.

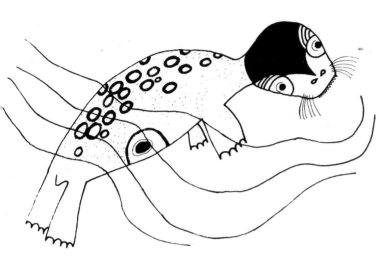

Below: The Anguit was a seal spirit that the Inuit of Kalaallit Nunaat (Greenland) worshipped.

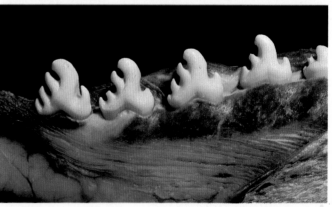

Below, top: Albrecht Dürer drew this picture of a walrus in 1521. Below, center: A modern photograph of a walrus. The walrus' tusks help it find food on the sea floor and protect it when fighting. Below, bottom: Crabeater seals feed on krill — small shrimp and sea crabs. Their teeth act like rakes. After a hearty bite, the tiny crabs stay in the seal's mouth, and the water flows out through spaces in the teeth.

44 pounds (22 kg) at birth. The mother seal nurses the pup for three to five days. She must finish before the ice floe melts. During this time, the pup's weight may double. This happens because the mother seal's milk is very fatty.

Not all seal pups have such a hectic birth. Harp seals and gray seals, for instance, stay with their mothers for several weeks. Their baby fur would not protect them in the water. But after nursing for two to three weeks, the pups have new fur, and the mother leaves them at this time to find a new mate.

Seal Families

Today there are thirty-three different kinds, or species, of seals in the world. Scientists divide seals into three major families. In one family are the "earless," or "true," seals. In another family are the "eared" seals — sea lions and fur seals. The last family has only one member, the walrus.

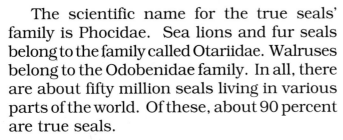

The scientific name for the true seals' family is Phocidae. Sea lions and fur seals belong to the family called Otariidae. Walruses belong to the Odobenidae family. In all, there are about fifty million seals living in various parts of the world. Of these, about 90 percent are true seals.

Diving and Eating

Seals are carnivores. This means they eat meat. In general, seals eat shellfish, mollusks, and many kinds of fish. But the leopard seal, for example, will also prey on penguins and, sometimes, even crabeater seals.

The seals' great diving ability helps them catch their prey. Dives of up to 1,970 feet (600 m) are common for many seals, and they can easily stay under water for twenty minutes or longer without coming back to the surface for air. On the other hand, the longest a human can stay under water is about two and a half minutes. Weddell seals have dived to depths of about 2,000 feet (600 m). They have stayed under water for over seventy minutes. The champion diver, however, is the elephant seal. It has dived more than 4,000 feet (1,220 m) deep.

Seals have special ways of keeping enough oxygen for their long dives. For one thing, seals have more blood cells than other mammals of the same size. Since blood carries the body's oxygen, this means seals have more oxygen. Also, seals' muscles can hold large stores of oxygen. A third reason why seals can dive so well has to do with which organs get the most blood. While diving, a seal's heartbeat slows down. Some body functions even stop. The important organs — the brain, the eyes, and the spinal cord — get enough oxygen, however. In this way, the seals can stay under water for a longer period of time.

People and Seals

Humans have hunted seals for tens of thousands of years. Cave paintings from the

Below: The collar of fat around the seal's neck acts as a float.

Bottom of page: When a harp seal mother hunts for food, she leaves her young behind on the ice. The mother here looks out of the ice hole to greet her pup.

Stone Age show men hunting seals. Over the years, the lives of the Inuit have depended on hunting seals. From the beginning, the Inuit used every part of the seals. The animals provided food and clothing, and tools were once made from bones. Oil from the blubber was burned in lamps that lit the long polar nights. One of the most important Inuit gods was Anguit, the spirit of the ringed seal.

Commercial hunting of seals began in the eighteenth century. The seal's fur and blubber oil were prized by European and American seal hunters. The number of seals killed climbed steadily, reaching a peak in the early 1900s. At that time, many species were close to extinction. Too many people wanted to wear the luxurious seal fur. Sealskin coats were very popular in the late 1940s, especially the white fur of the baby harp seal.

Scientists in Canada started measuring the seal population around 1950. They counted the number of seals that were born. Then they compared that number against the number of seals that were being killed each year. They found that the seal populations were in terrible danger. But progress in stopping the senseless slaughter of seals was slow. It was not until about 1970 that limits were placed on how many seals could be killed in the world each year. Fortunately, by the mid-1980s, the numbers of seals killed were well below the allowed quotas. During

Sea lions are born with an excellent sense of balance, so many difficult tricks are easy for them. Training often provides a welcome challenge for these intelligent animals.

Below, left: California sea lions perform a balancing act at the Basler Zoo.
Below, right: A trainer from Schweitzer National Circus with California sea lions.

this decade, the general public was made aware of and educated about the plight of the seals. This was due in large part to the work of various animal conservation groups around the world. Through the efforts of concerned activists working together for the welfare of these beautiful animals, the numbers of most species of seals are increasing.

Seal Records

Largest: the southern elephant seal male can grow to be 16.5 feet (5 m) long and weigh 8,818 pounds (4,000 kg).

Smallest: the Baikal seal.

Largest population: the crabeater seal species has about 30 million animals.

Fastest in the water: the California sea lion swims at about 25 miles per hour (40 kph).

Fastest on land: the crabeater seal. It runs at 15.5 miles per hour (25 kph) over the ice.

Deepest dive: the northern elephant seal has dived over 4,000 feet (1220 m) deep.

Longest underwater: Weddell seals can stay underwater more than 70 minutes.

Longest living: a ringed seal lived to be 46 years old.

Longest intestine: of all the nursed animals, the southern elephant seal has the longest intestine, which is 42 times longer than its body. Many of these seals are a part of an organ donor program.

Largest group of nursing pups in the world: the northern fur seals on the Pribilof Islands, Alaska. Over the year, more than one million animals gather here.

Mediterranean Monk Seal

Southern Elephant Seal

Harbor Seal

A Guide to *Seals*

Australian Sea Lions

Northern Fur Seal

Walrus

Harbor Seals

Scientific name: Phoca vitulina
Length: 5-6 feet (1.5-2 m)
Weight: 165-250 pounds (75-113 kg)

southern coasts of Greenland and Iceland. There are also harbor seals in the northern Atlantic Ocean, stretching up along the coast of Norway.

Harbor seals prefer flat, sandy shores that have sandbanks. But they also like shingle beaches and rocky shorelines that

The harbor seal, also called the common seal or the spotted seal, is the best-known and loved of all the seals. Its coat is basically a gray or brownish gray color, liberally sprinkled with small black spots that rarely blend into solid patches of any kind. There is no apparent color difference between the males and females of the species. Harbor seals have a short, round head and nostrils that are set in a wide "V" pattern.

The harbor seal lives along the east coast of Asia near Japan and then spreads across the Pacific Ocean to Alaska and then down the west coasts of Canada and the United States. It also lives along the east coasts of the United States and Canada and the

gradually shelve into the water. There, they can sunbathe on the rocky areas or dive into the ocean to hunt for food. For example, they like the Wadden Sea, which is off the coast of northern Germany, near the mouth of the Elbe River. Harbor seals sometimes swim up rivers. In fact, the zoologist Erna Mohr reported that the harbor seal has been seen swimming about 435 miles (700 km) up the Elbe. In Hamburg, about 45 miles (72 km) up the Elbe, the seals are seen regularly. Before the Elbe became polluted, many more seals were seen there.

Baby seals are born between February and September, depending on where the seal lives. The expectant harbor seal female searches for a remote, quiet sandbank on which to give birth.

At birth, the harbor seal is about 30 inches (80 cm) long and weighs about 22 pounds (10 kg). This baby seal, called a *pup*, is covered with a white fur coat that changes to a normal grayish color after a short period

the cry of a human baby. If its mother cannot find the pup, other females will not take care of it; they will feed only their own offspring, and a lost pup will probably starve. But the seal mother can recognize her pup's body odor and distinctive voice among the other seal pups.

of time. The pup is ready to swim only a few hours after birth. The seal mother is very devoted to her baby at first and nurses the pup for four to six weeks. During that time she pays close attention to the pup, defending it from any possible attack and protecting it from getting lost in the sea. Sometimes, especially during a storm, a young seal wanders away from its mother and is lost. It lets out screams that sound something like

Above, left: The shy northern Atlantic (North Sea) harbor seals are rarely observed at such a close range. Above, right: A lost seal pup will cry all day long for its mother. Fortunately, a mother seal can recognize her pup's cry.
Right: Harbor seals nurse only their own young.

After about six weeks, the young seal, like the adults, will eat fish, cuttlefish, crabs, shrimp, and plankton. Seals use their eyes to hunt for food under water as well as on land. Their eyes are very sensitive and can see well even in dim or unclear light. During a full moon, for example, seals can see

this theory, the seals' well developed hearing helps them locate prey. For example, the seal makes clicking sounds that bounce off other sea animals. The sounds alert the seal to the slightest bit of movement and help it detect the location of prey with great accuracy. Using its whiskers, the seal then moves along

Harbor seals move almost weightlessly in the water. They propel themselves with their rear flippers and use their front flippers to steer. Sea lions and fur seals, on the other hand, propel themselves with their front flippers.

movement about 1,300 feet (400 m) below the surface of water, and the skillful harbor seals can even catch their prey in darkness. Some scientists believe that harbor seals also have a kind of sonar hearing system. According to

the sea bottom, and when the prey moves, the seal grabs it. This hunting method, which may also apply to California sea lions and Steller's sea lions, works best when the prey is about 20 inches (50 cm) away.

The breeding cycle of the harbor seals in the northeastern Atlantic Ocean is typical of most harbor seals. In August and September, the harbor seal changes its fur. This process is called *molting*. The quiet time during molting takes place just before the mating season, which begins toward the end of September. Then, the usually quiet seals become excited. Like dolphins, some male seals even leap out of the water in spectacular jumps. After mating, the seals splash and paddle through the water together, and in late fall, the seals leave the beach area. Scientists once thought they went to the deep sea to fish over the winter. But a German researcher attached small radio transmitters to the fur of some harbor seals, and he proved that they did not go into the open sea. Rather, they went to the rim of the Wadden Sea, where they could remain hidden from the shore. There, the seals had shallow water and sandbanks, where they could rest after fishing trips.

At one time, seal hunting reduced the number of harbor seals to about one thousand. Laws limiting the number of seals that could be killed were successful in again increasing the seal population, but the harbor seal now has to cope with the problems of water pollution. The materials that humans dump into the world's major waterways and pollute the once-pristine waters can be harmful to all sea animals. An example of how serious the problem can be happened in 1988. In the summer of that year, a mysterious epidemic struck the harbor seals of the northern Atlantic. Thousands of dead seals washed up on the beaches. About 80 percent of the entire seal population in the Wadden Sea died. Seals in nearby areas where the water was cleaner did not get sick, and it now seems that the seals are safe from catching the disease. Perhaps the population will return to what it once was.

Largha Seals

Scientific name: Phoca largha
Length: females, 4.6-5.2 feet (1.4-1.6 m);
*   males, 5.2-5.6 feet (1.6-1.7 m)*
Weight: 175-220 pounds (80-100 kg)

The largha seals, also called spotted seals, live in the Pacific Ocean from Japan to the Bering Sea and on to northern Alaska. The young, however, are born only on the solid ice in the far north, mainly in the Chukchi, Okhotsk, and Bering seas.

At one time, scientists thought that the largha seal and harbor seal were the same species. With their dark spots on a silver background, the two do look like each other. Largha seals, however, are quite a bit smaller than the harbor seals, and they give birth to their young only on ice. Harbor seal pups are born on sandbanks and small rocky islands.

Largha seals usually pair off during mating season, and the seal couples stay together for about two months. During this mating time, each seal couple tries to stay away from other such pairs.

Although time of birth can vary slightly in different geographical areas, young larghas are usually born in spring, warmly wrapped in their white fur, or *lanugo*. This wooly baby coat is shed two to four weeks after birth, when the baby has a new coat of pale silver covered with dark spots. Unlike the pups of other kinds of seals, the young largha seals do not start swimming immediately. The ice is a dry place where they stay during the nursing period. Nursing lasts from two to six weeks, and during this time, the pups usually triple their birth weight. The largha babies are about 32 inches (82 cm) long and weigh about 15 to 22 pounds (7-10 kg). After nursing, they may weigh as much as 62 pounds (28 kg). It is estimated that there are about 400,000 largha seals in the world.

Ringed Seals

Scientific name: Phoca hispida
Length: 4.6-4.9 feet (1.4-1.5 m)
Weight: 110 pounds (50 kg)

In the fall, when the ice blanket is forming, it is very important that the seals keep the air hole open. And the ringed seal is a master at this skill. When a thin sheet of ice forms, the seal pushes its snout or heavy fore-flipper through the ice. In the cold, Arctic weather, a new sheet of ice forms over the hole. The

The ringed seal is the most common seal in the Arctic region.

There are about six to seven million ringed seals in the world. They are the second most common of the true seals. They get their name from the light rings on the dark fur on their backs. The ringed seal is found in a broad region around the North Pole. The seals are born on the ice, and they hunt along the fish-rich area on the edge of the ice blanket. Ringed seals can dive up to 295 feet (90 m) deep on a hunt for fish. They come up for air to a hole they have made in the ice.

seal then breaks the new sheet. Each time the hole freezes over, the seal breaks the ice. Finally, even though the ice has become about 6.5 feet (2 m) thick, the air hole is open.

Later, when snow falls, the ringed seal comes through its hole and digs a kind of room for itself in the snow. The snow helps protect the seals from storms and from polar foxes and bears. A polar bear can actually smell a seal through the snow. It can then break in and reach the tasty meal. Once the snow gets about 6.5 feet (2 m) deep, however, the bears cannot get in.

In March and April, the female seal gives birth to her pup in the snow den. The den can only be entered through the water. The pups weigh from 9 to 11 pounds (4-5 kg). The mother nurses the pups for almost two months. After about two weeks, the pups molt. They trade their long, white baby fur for a wonderful, waterproof coat of silver fur. The pups swim for the first time when they are about four to six weeks old. They still stay close to their mother, however.

The ringed seal has a thicker layer of blubber than most seals. Up to half its weight can be blubber. The ringed seal has been hunted by the Inuit. This large amount of fat helps keeps the seal afloat after it has died, a fact that has made the job of the Inuit hunters easy. For many years, life for the Inuit in the far north would have been impossible without the ringed seal. The meat was, for a long time, the main food of the Inuit. The fat was used for cooking and for lamp oil; the fur was made into boots and clothing.

Caspian and Baikal Seals

Scientific name: Caspian, Phoca caspica
    Baikal, Phoca sibirica
Length: both, up to 4 feet (1.25 m)
Weight: Caspian, 55 pounds (24 kg)
    Baikal, 72 pounds (32 kg)

The Caspian and Baikal seals are close relatives of the ringed seal. The Caspian seal lives only in the Caspian Sea. The seals always stay where the water is the coldest. In the winter, it is coldest in the northern part of the sea. In the north, however, the ice melts in the summer. Then the seals move back to the southern end, where the water is deeper and cooler. Special laws forbid killing female seals during breeding season, along with

pregnant females or baby seals. Today, there are about 500,000 to 600,000 Caspian seals. Mating season is between the end of February and the middle of March, and pups are usually born in late January. Their main enemies are wolves and eagles.

The Baikal seal is a small seal that feeds mainly on fish in Lake Baikal.

The Baikal seal is found only in Lake Baikal in Siberia, near the Mongolian border. Lake Baikal is a freshwater lake — the deepest lake in the world. Pups are born from late February through March on the ice in special little snow houses called *lairs.* At first, the pups have a white lanugo coat, but they soon shed this woolly coat for a smooth, dark gray one. Today, there are about fifty thousand Baikal seals.

Harp Seals

Scientific name: Phoca groenlandica
Length: up to 5.2 feet (1.6 m)
Weight: 298 pounds (135 kg)

There are three main groups of harp seals. One is in the White Sea. Another is east of Greenland near Jan Mayen Island. The third is off Newfoundland near the coast of Canada. The best-known of the harp seal colonies is the one near Newfoundland. That is where the females meet in February to search for a

The harp seal is also called the saddleback or Greenland seal. It leads a busy life, and a fair amount of its time is spent migrating. The harp seal is a nimble swimmer and can jump out of the water the way dolphins do. In the summer, the harp seal travels as far as the northernmost areas of the Atlantic Ocean. This area is a good place to hunt for cod, herring, and carp.

In the fall, harp seals travel south. During this time, they form large herds, mate, and bring their young into the world.

place on the pack ice to have their pups. The harp female prefers a place where the thick ice is cracked with rough edges and spaces. The rocky ice offers some protection against enemies and the weather.

For the young harp seal, being born must be a shock. It comes from the warmth of its mother's body to the wind and ice and temperatures of near 5° F (-15° C). The pups weigh about 13-22 pounds (6-10 kg) at birth. They nurse for seven to twelve days and gain about 4.5-5.5 pounds (10-12 kg) each day. After nursing, the mother leaves the pup to mate again. The harp seal pups stay on the ice for another two weeks. Then they molt and get their thick, waterproof adult fur. By this time, the pups have a thick layer of blubber to protect them from the icy conditions and can hunt on their own. They eat small crabs until they are able to catch fish.

The harp seal almost became extinct because of its white baby fur. Fur trappers killed thousands of newborn pups each year to get the valuable fur. But the United States and the countries of Europe stopped allowing the fur to be imported. For the most part, this stopped the killing.

The older harp seals gather on an ice floe in April and May to molt. During molting, they rarely go into the water. Once they have their new coats, they begin traveling again. In June, most harp seals can be found in Greenland in the areas that have a lot of fish.

Opposite page: These ice fields are the birthplace of the harp seals. Because of their wonderful fur, thousands of these harp seal pups were once slaughtered.

Ribbon Seals

Scientific name: Phoca fasciata
Length: 4.9 feet (1.5 m)
Weight: 198 pounds (90 kg)

Ribbon seals are close relatives of the harp seals. Their dark brown bodies have yellow-white bands around their lower backs, flippers, and necks. The ribbon seal's territory reaches from northern Japan to the Okhotsk, Bering, and Chukchi seas.

Scientists do not know very much about the ribbon seals, but their life seems to be similar to that of the harp seal. Young ribbon seals are born on the ice in April and early May. At first they have white fur, but they generally lose this baby fur at the age of five weeks. The pups nurse for three to four weeks, and during this time they gain between 22 and 66 pounds (10-30 kg). They are then left by their mothers, who go on to mate again and to molt. Scientists estimate the average life span of the ribbon seals as being about twenty years.

The ribbon seal is a close relative of the harp seal and lives only in the North Pacific.

Gray Seals

Scientific name: Halichoerus grypus
Length: females, up to 6.2 feet (1.9 m);
   males, up to 7.2 feet (2.2 m)
Weight: females, up to 331 pounds (150 kg);
   males, up to 660 pounds (300 kg)

mid-December to mid-February, and the Baltic young are born in February and March.

Male and female gray seals are different from each other in appearance. Males are much larger than females and are dark with light spots. Females have a lighter background color with darker spots. The stronger male gray seals usually stay with six or seven

The gray seal lives in temperate and subarctic seas on both sides of the North Atlantic. It has a long, pointed snout, a strong bite, and a powerful build. There are three main groups of gray seals. One group lives in the western Atlantic Ocean off the coast of Canada. Another lives in the eastern Atlantic near the coasts of Great Britain, Iceland, and Norway. The third group lives in the Baltic Sea.

The young of each group of gray seals are born at different times of the year. The eastern Atlantic seals are born in fall and early winter, western Atlantic pups are born

females. They will fight to keep other nearby males away.

Gray seals are mainly fish eaters and seem to like all types. Scientists have recorded at least twenty-nine different types of fish eaten by these seals. They also eat mollusks and some crustaceans. Today, there are about 120,000 gray seals in the world.

Above: Gray seals live on the rocky coastlines of the North Atlantic. Their coat colors vary and can be any shade of gray, brown, and silver.

Hooded Seals

Scientific name: Cystophora cristata
Length: females, up to 7.2 feet (2.2 m);
    males, up to 8.8 feet (2.7 m)
Weight: females, up to 772 pounds (350 kg);
    males, up to 882 pounds (400 kg)

The hooded seal has a strange shape. It gets its name from the skin sac, or hood, that the male has on the top of its head. He can blow up the skin sac to about twice the size of a soccer ball. The male hooded seal can perform another amazing trick. He can inflate the skin from the inside of his nostril. It looks like a red balloon coming out of the opening.

Hooded seals live in the northwestern Atlantic Ocean near Greenland and

The most remarkable feature of the male hooded seal is the inflatable hood on top of its head.

Newfoundland. Pups are born on the ice. After the female gives birth, the male stays with her and helps protect the pup from enemies. This behavior is seldom found among seals.

In the seal colonies in Newfoundland, the young are born in the spring when the ice begins to break apart. The mother nurses her pup for only three to five days. During this time, the pup doubles its weight from about 45 to 90 pounds (20-40 kg).

Bearded Seals

Scientific name: Erignathus barbatus
Length: up to 7.4 feet (2.25 m)
Weight: up to 573 pounds (260 kg)

The bearded seal uses its moustache to help it sense and search for food.

The adult male bearded seal has what looks like a droopy, messy beard with a moustache. All this hair has many nerve endings, which make the seals sensitive to touching things. The sensitive hair endings help the seals find small crabs, snails, mussels, sea pickles, and worms along the ocean floor. Because the bearded seal searches on the sea floor for food, it prefers still waters. These large sea animals are found in the icy area surrounding the North Pole.

Bearded seals give birth to their young in the spring on ice packs that float in Arctic and subarctic waters. They nurse their babies between twelve and eighteen days. During this time, the seal pups already learn to eat small crabs.

Bearded seals are hunted by the Inuit for their valuable fur. At one time, the seal's skin was used to make window panes, sled thongs, whips, and hunting lines. There are about 500,000 bearded seals in the world today.

Mediterranean Monk Seals

Scientific name: Monachus monachus
Length: females, up to 9.8 feet (3 m);
* males, up to 9.5 feet (2.9 m)*
Weight: up to 882 pounds (400 kg)

At one time, there were three types of monk seals. The Mediterranean monk seal lived on all the coasts of the Mediterranean Sea, on the Black Sea, and on the northwest coast of Africa. The Caribbean monk seal lived in the Caribbean Sea between Cuba and South America. The Hawaiian monk seal

The Mediterranean monk seal survives today on only a few beaches.

Aristotle, Homer, Pliny, and other ancient Greeks wrote about the Mediterranean monk seal. People ate their flesh, used their fat, and thought the seal's body brought magical powers. The Romans, for instance, believed that sealskin shoes protected them from getting gout. The Mediterranean monk seal's right flipper was placed under a pillow to cure sleeplessness. Some people also believed that a tent made from the monk seal's skin would provide protection in a lightning storm.

lived in the Hawaiian Islands. Today, the Caribbean monk seal is probably extinct, since none of these seals have been seen for about forty years. To make matters worse, there are fewer than fifteen hundred Hawaiian monk seals and five hundred Mediterranean monk seals.

The Mediterranean monk seal, more than any other seal, does not like to live near people. In the past, these seals liked to spend time on the sandy beaches. Now, the human population of their areas has grown to about two hundred million. During the summer, another two hundred million people come there on vacation. There is no more room on the beaches for the seals. The Mediterranean monk seals still surviving live on the coasts of Turkey, Greece, and North Africa. They hunt seal may be so disturbed that she will abandon her pup. In addition to all their other problems, the Mediterranean monk seals are affected by the harmful materials in the polluted waters.

The World Wildlife Foundation and other groups have been working to save these seals. One plan is to create special areas, called

Hawaiian monk seals (above), like the Mediterranean monks, are easily affected by disturbances from people.

for food during the day and hide at night. They live in grottoes and caves that they enter from underground tunnels. The young are born in these caves.

Even in the caves, the Mediterranean monk seals are not safe. Many fishermen believe the seals eat too many fish and so try to kill the seals. Also, curious divers sometimes enter the seal caves. If a diver arrives during the six-week nursing period, it can have terrible consequences. The mother *reserves*, where the seals will be safe from human destruction.

The future of the Hawaiian monk seal does not look very good. These seals give birth to their young on open beach areas. They, too, are nervous near humans. Accidental meetings with people can disturb the mother seal and cause her to abandon her pup. This means, of course, that the young monk seal has no one to provide for or protect it, and it will soon starve.

Weddell Seals

Scientific name: Leptonychotes weddelli
Length: up to 9.8 feet (3 m)
Weight: up to 1,100 pounds (500 kg)

the pups are about 3 feet (1 m) long and weigh 55 pounds (25 kg). For the first two weeks, the mother and pups stay together on the ice. But toward the end of the sixth or seventh week of nursing, they can both often be seen in the waters.

Weddell seals live mainly on fish, and they

Weddell seals are not very social, and they gather together only to mate. These seals prefer the deep sea, where they sometimes dive deeper than 1,970 feet (600 m).

The Weddell seal is one of four seal species that live in a ring around the southern ice continent of Antarctica. The other three are the crabeater, leopard, and Ross seals. All four species eat different foods and live in different areas. Weddell seals are the largest of the four species, and most are found on solid ice that can be seen from the coast.

Groups of females gather when it is time to give birth to pups. Weddell pups are born from August through November. At birth,

hunt at a depth of almost 2,000 feet (610 m). Their diving ability is amazing. In fact, the Weddell seal can stay under water for as long as seventy minutes. To understand this seal's incredible diving ability, one must know what happens during a long, deep dive. A person would probably become unconscious on a dive as deep as that of a Weddell seal. The brain would not get enough oxygen, and the lungs would release nitrogen into the blood. Then air in the brain would compress, and blood cells would burst. During a rapid dive, the human body would act something like a soda can that is opened quickly. That could kill the person.

An American researcher discovered how the Weddell seal can make its dives. He reports that, for their size, Weddell seals have twice the number of blood cells that a human has. This means that the seal's blood cells can somehow hold more oxygen than a human's. To discover this, the researchers attached instruments and a small computer to a seal's back. They could then watch the seal's body functions during the deep dives.

Before a seal dives, it breathes out. It uses oxygen from its blood and muscles on the downward journey. At a depth of about 130 to 165 feet (40-50 m), the lungs become completely compressed from the water pressure. The last air in the lungs is pressed back into the windpipe. This means that no dangerous nitrogen can get into the bloodstream from the lungs.

After the first part of the dive, the seal's heartbeat slows down. At this point, blood does not go to most of the organs. This saves oxygen. At the same time, oxygen that is stored in the muscles is released. Only the brain, eyes, and other sense organs continue to receive blood and oxygen. These organs need to operate so the seal can find its way back to the surface of the water.

Researchers in this study concluded that during the first fifteen minutes of the dive, the number of blood cells in the seal's blood increases. These blood cells then act like a diver's air tank. The extra cells get into the seal's system as they are needed.

Weddell seals feed mainly on fish, but they will also eat squid and some crustaceans. Their natural enemies are leopard seals and killer whales, but they are curious rather than frightened or angered by contact with humans. Scientists estimate the Weddell seal world population at about 800,000.

Left: Weddell seals are solitary animals. They live among the ice floes of their Antarctic environment and come up between spaces in the ice to breathe.

Crabeater Seals

Scientific name: Lobodon carcinophagus
Length: up to 8.5 feet (2.6 m)
Weight: up to 496 pounds (225 kg)

Almost the entire diet of the crabeater seal consists of *krill* — small shrimp and crablike animals that travel together in large quantities. To eat, the hungry crabeater seal only has to open its mouth as it swims into a school of krill. The seal then closes its mouth and forces the water out through its teeth. Only

Crabeater seals are the most abundant seals in the world.

Its long, lanky body and pointed snout make the crabeater seal easy to identify. There are more crabeater seals in the world than any other kind of seal. About thirty-five million of the seals live along the icy borders of Antarctica, where they breed on the ice floes surrounding the coastline. Pups are born in the Antarctic spring, from about September to early November, and the fur at birth is a pale coffee color. Experts believe the mother seals nurse their pups for about four weeks.

the shrimp and crabs are left inside its mouth. The crabeaters have well-developed, comblike teeth that are specially suited to their diet. These seals eat the same way that some whales and the emperor penguin do. Sometimes, these seals will also eat squid and small quantities of fish.

Because of the abundance of the crabeater seals, it has been difficult for scientists to estimate their numbers. But there is no doubt that the population is very large.

Leopard Seals

Scientific name: Hydrurga leptonyx
*Length: females, up to 11.8 feet (3.6 m);
   males, up to 9.8 feet (3 m)*
*Weight: females, up to 794 pounds (360 kg);
   males, up to 728 pounds (330 kg)*

The head of the solitary leopard seal gives it a reptilian look.

Leopard seals, with their distinctive spotted neck and large head, are very striking seals. They are found only on the icy coasts of Antarctica, and scientists believe there are about 440,000 of the animals in the world. Leopard seals do not prey on humans, but they cannot be considered harmless, as there has been at least one report of a leopard seal attacking a human. The leopards may react violently to being disturbed by other seals, and other seals have been seen jumping out of the water and running across the ice to escape a chasing leopard seal.

Leopard seals have a varied diet. They prey on many species of penguins, as well as on young crabeater, Weddell, and elephant seals. They also feed on fish and crabs. They catch penguins under the water and drag them onto the ice to eat them.

Experts know very little about how leopard seals reproduce. The pups are probably born sometime between September and January and weigh 55 to 66 pounds (25-30 kg).

Ross Seals

Scientific name: Ommatophoca rossi
*Length: females, up to 8.2 feet (2.5 m);
   males, up to 9.8 feet (3 m)*
Weight: 440-463 pounds (200-210 kg)

Among all seals, scientists know the least about the Ross seals. They have gray backs and silver-white undersides, with giant eyes that are in striking contrast to their small mouths. Ross seals live solitary lives on the ice floes around Antarctica. There are about 220,000 of these animals in the world.

The Ross seal's main foods are cuttlefish, squid, and krill. In order to catch these fast-moving prey, the Ross seals must be good swimmers. Their sharp eyes help them see in the dark water under the thick Antarctic ice blanket. The shape of their teeth helps them hold onto the slippery cuttlefish.

Almost nothing is known about how the Ross seals reproduce, but their solitary habits indicate that they might breed in pairs rather than in large groups. An examination of an unborn pup in its mother's womb suggested that it would be born in late November or early December.

Southern Elephant Seals

Scientific name: Mirounga leonina
Length: females, up to 9.8 feet (3 m);
*   males, up to 16.4 feet (5 m)*
Weight: females, up to 1,984 pounds
*   (900 kg); males, up to 8,818 pounds*
*   (4,000 kg)*

not as long as a land elephant's, but it still makes a mighty trumpet sound. The snout, or trunk, on adult elephant bulls grows from the front of the mouth. Their nostrils point downward into the mouth.

During mating season, the trunk puffs up with air similar to the way the sacs of the

A southern elephant seal roars with its trunk in the air.

The southern elephant seal lives around the South Pole and on nearby islands. Its main mating grounds lie south of South America, Africa, and Australia. The southern elephant seal is the largest seal in the world. This colossal animal is even bigger than the mighty walrus, which is only half its weight. In September, during mating season, the elephant bulls fill the air with their roaring; they use their snouts to make the roaring sound louder. An elephant bull's snout is

hooded seal do. Adult elephant seal males fight hard to become the leader of a group of females. The bulls attack each other's necks and shoulders; all bulls have deep scars from these fights. Their necks look very much like the bark of a very old tree. A bull first fights for a group of females, called a *harem*, at the age of eight. The harems usually have twenty to forty females, although some harems can have up to one hundred females. Only harem bulls mate, and not every male becomes a harem bull; so some southern elephant seals live their whole lives without mating. A bull usually lives for twelve years, but some may reach the age of twenty.

Life for the female elephant seal is not easy, either. In October of each year, a group of females go to land to give birth to their back to the sea to eat. All in all, the process of mating, gestation, and birth takes just over one year.

At this point, the elephant seal pups are left behind on land, so they gather into groups. Since they still cannot go into the sea, their food is their own fat and the small crabs they

What looks like a mother with her arm around her pup is really a southern elephant seal couple. The elephant seal bull lies next to a female that is only a fraction of his size.

pups. Each group is led by one bull. After the birth, the females stay with their pups and nurse their young for about three weeks. During that time, the females do not eat. By the end of the nursing period, the pups are gaining about 20 pounds (9 kg) per day. By this time, the female has lost about 700 pounds (320 kg). In about three weeks, the female will leave the pups to mate again. By the end of November, the difficult time is over. The adults leave the pups and crawl

may catch on the shore. About ten days after birth, the pups begin to molt. It takes about three weeks for them to get their new adult fur. Molting is painful for the pups, since scraps of dry skin are lost with the baby fur. In addition, molting causes itching. Sometimes the pups dig themselves into mud to relieve the irritation from molting. Finally, when the pups are just over one month old, the molting is complete. They are ready to start their lives in the sea.

Northern Elephant Seals

Scientific name: Mirounga angustirostris
Length: females, up to 11.8 feet (3.6 m);
*   males, up to 14.8 feet (4.5 m)*
Weight: females, up to 1,984 pounds (900 kg);
*   males, up to 5,513 pounds (2,500 kg)*

The northern elephant seal lives along the coasts of California and Mexico. It was probably discovered in the northern Pacific Ocean in 1775. At that time, it was rarely hunted by humans, since fur seals brought more money. By the beginning of the 1800s, however, people realized that the elephant seal had a thick layer of blubber. The layer was about 6 inches (15 cm) thick and made up about 40 percent of the adult male's

A northern elephant seal bull relaxes in the sun with his trunk hanging over the body of a female elephant seal.

weight. About 45 to 68 gallons (170-260 l) of oil could be taken from the blubber of each animal. Hunters then showed no mercy. Like many other kinds of seals, large numbers of the northern elephant seals were killed. By 1885, hundreds of herds had disappeared.

It is fortunate that the northern elephant seals did not become extinct. A small colony

of fewer than one hundred animals survived near the island of Guadalupe, off the western coast of Mexico. Then, in 1892, this last herd was discovered, and fourteen of the animals were shot to send to museums. Luckily, the Mexican government stepped in. It quickly put this last herd under its protection.

Since then, the animals have been steadily multiplying. Today, there are probably about 120,000 northern elephant seals. Their population is still increasing, but there is some doubt that it can continue. Since today's animals come from so few ancestors, the animals are somewhat weak. The future of the northern elephant seal is shaky.

The mating and birth times of the northern elephant seal are similar to those of the southern elephant seals. The bull must fight bloody battles to gain a harem. Higher ranking males take over the others' beaches. Harem males are challenged every December, at the beginning of the birthing time.

twenty-seven days to nurse and gain weight. At birth, the pups weigh about 100 pounds (45 kg). By the end of the nursing period, their weight will probably have tripled. It can, however, increase as many as seven times. During the nursing period, the mother does not eat. At the end of this time, the mother is

Two northern elephant seal bulls in the middle of a fight over a group of females.

The trunk, or *proboscis*, of the male hangs about 12 inches (30 cm) over its mouth. When the bull roars, the sounds are pushed through the trunk and into the mouth, where they are strengthened. The roar can be heard almost one mile away.

Northern elephant seal pups are born in late December to mid-March, covered with a curly, black baby coat. They stay on land for

very weak, so she immediately crawls back to the ocean and dives to the floor to eat. Most of the females feed at depths of about 1,150 to 2,133 feet (350-650 m) under the sea. They eat mainly fish and squid.

A northern elephant seal holds the seal diving record. It reached a depth of 4,101 feet (1,250 m). Even the Weddell seal cannot dive this deep.

California Sea Lions

Scientific name: Zalophus californianus
Length: females, 5.9 feet (1.8 m);
   males, 7.2 feet (2.2 m)
Weight: females, 220 -250 pounds (100-115
   kg); males, 600-750 pounds (272-340 kg)

California sea lions are intelligent animals that train easily. Each behavior learned depends on both the difficulty of the activity and the personality of the animal.

In zoos, sea lions usually eat fish. In the wild, they still enjoy fish but will also eat octopus and squid. There are usually many

The California sea lion bull (middle animal) with his forehead bulge is easy to recognize.

California sea lions are the best-known of the eared seal family. Almost everyone has seen their balancing act at a zoo or a circus. Balancing seems to be natural to the California sea lions. These peace-loving sea lions also sometimes try to catch their own air bubbles underwater. As their name suggests, they live mainly on the coasts of southern California and western Mexico.

salmon in the waters where the sea lions live. However, the sea lion prefers eating the lamprey eels that live off the salmon.

The reproduction period begins in May for the California sea lions. First, the males search for a suitable place to mate on land. The territory should ideally have a path close to the shoreline with easy access to the sea so that the males can go into the water and cool off from time to time. California sea lions are not real fighters; instead, the bulls claim or defend their area by roaring and barking. The roar sounds like that of a lion, which is how the sea lion got its name. Every two weeks, the bulls go into the water to eat. When they return, they must fight again to claim a new territory.

The females gradually arrive on the land to bear their young from the previous mating season. Several cows will form a harem and stay in the area of one bull. For two or three days, the newborn pup is closely guarded by the mother. She even takes her pup with her

Steller's Sea Lions

Scientific name: Eumetopias jubatus
Length: females, up to 7.2 feet (2.2 m);
males, up to 9.8 feet (3 m)
Weight: females, up to 595 pounds (270 kg);
males, up to 2,200 pounds (1,000 kg)

Steller's sea lion is the largest of the sea lions and lives in the northern Pacific Ocean. The animal was named for a German nature researcher, George William Steller, who discovered them in 1800. Steller's sea lions

A Steller's sea lion bull with his harem. These sea lions are very social animals.

for the first few days when she goes into the sea to eat. After the first few days, however, the mother sea lion moves farther away from the pup when in the water.

Meanwhile, the pups gather together in groups to play. Two weeks after the young are born, the female is ready to mate with the harem bull. After fifty weeks, another pup will be born.

have a lifestyle similar to the California sea lion. They are more aggressive, however. To claim a territory, bulls have fierce fights.

After the birth of a pup, the mother staunchly defends her young against other sea lions and people. Mother and pup stay together much longer than other sea lions do. The pup often nurses until the next young is born about a year later.

Southern Sea Lions

Scientific name: Otaria byronia
Length: females, about 6.5 feet (2 m);
*   males, about 8.2 feet (2.5 m)*
Weight: females, about 330 pounds (150 kg);
*   males, 660-1,146 pounds (300-520 kg)*

The southern sea lion lives along the coast of South America from Peru to Tierra del Fuego to the Falkland Islands to Uruguay. It is also called the South American sea lion. The male sea lion has what can be called a mane on its massive throat and neck. This hair is often a different color from the rest of its coat.

Each year until August, the southern sea lion bulls mainly eat and rest. Then, in August, they become active and claim territories that they fiercely defend. Like other male sea lions, the bull has a group of females called a harem. At first, the bull does not mate because so much time is spent defending its territory. But once the young from the previous mating season are born, and the females have left these pups, a new mating season begins. At this point, the females do not go back to the sea until they have mated with the bull.

The gestation period for the southern sea lion is about one year. Once all the cows have mated, the harem splits up. Then the bull, who has not eaten for many weeks, can return to the sea to eat.

The mother sea lions also go to the sea to eat, but they return to nurse their young.

The southern sea lion male can be recognized by its mane; both males and females have upward-pointed snouts.

Like all sea lions and most other seals, a mother can recognize her young by its scent and voice. A female will not nurse another's pup, so a sea lion pup separated from its mother will starve. When the mothers leave to eat, the pups gather into groups to play. They do not go into the water alone at first, but they later follow their mothers into the sea. As soon as the pair gets to deep water, the pup climbs to safety on its mother's back.

Southern sea lions eat the same food that other sea lions do — fish, squid, and octopus. They also like little crabs called *Munida.* On the Falkland Islands, the southern sea lions are known as robbers because they eat southern fur seal females and pups. They also prey on penguins.

Today, there are about 270,000 southern sea lions in the world, but their numbers seem to be going down.

A slender, silvery gray female Australian sea lion scratches her chin with a back flipper.

Australian and New Zealand Sea Lions

Scientific name: Australian, Neophoca cinerea
New Zealand, Phocarctos hookeri
Length: females, 4.9 feet (1.5 m);
males, 6.6 feet (2 m)
Weight: females, 220 pounds (100 kg);
males, 660 pounds (300 kg)

The Australian sea lion is found only on the southern coast of Australia. Males are larger than females, and each bull fights for a group of females for its harem. The male Australian sea lion treats the females roughly, and sometimes the young pups, too.

The reproductive cycle of the Australian sea lion differs from all other sea lions. Other sea lions give birth to their young at the same time each year. The Australian sea lion female, on the other hand, has a range of four months in which she gives birth. Then there is an eighteen-month space between births, so a birth always comes every other year. The Australian sea lion mother stays with her new baby and nurses it for fourteen days. Then she crawls back to the ocean to eat. After this time, the mother leaves periodically to feed herself, but she still nurses her pups for twelve to twenty-four months. The life of the young sea lion is not easy, and the Australian sea lion can be very aggressive. Sometimes a sleeping pup is bitten, knocked, or thrown into the air by a harem bull, a half-grown male, or even a fierce female.

The New Zealand, or Auckland, sea lion lives only near the Auckland and Campbell islands just south of New Zealand. This sea lion is more peaceful than its Australian relative. The male, for example, treats the females and young much better. Both species feed on fish and cuttlefish. Occasionally, they will catch and eat penguins.

Southern Fur Seals

Scientific name: Arctocephalus pusillus
Length: females, 5.9 feet (1.8 m);
   males, 7.5 feet (2.3 m)
Weight: females, up to 220 pounds (100 kg);
   males, up to 660 pounds (300 kg)

Islands. Population: 30,000. **South American fur seals** (*A. australis*) live along the coasts of South America. Population: 500,000. **New Zealand fur seals** (*A. forsteri*) live along the rocky coasts of New Zealand. Population: 55,000. **Antarctic fur seals** (*A. gazella*) live on islands between the South Pole, Africa, and South America. Population: 1,200,000.

A male South African fur seal is the obvious center of attention in this breeding colony.

Southern fur seals are a group of eight species of seals. These seals can live as far north as Mexico, but most live near Antarctica on the southern coasts of Australia, South America, and Africa.

Guadalupe fur seals (*Arctocephalus townsendi*) live on Guadalupe Island in Mexico. Population: 2,500. **Juan Fernandez fur seals** (*A. philippii*) live on islands near Chile. Population: 6,300. **Galapagos fur seals** (*A. galapagoensis*) live on the Galapagos

Subantarctic fur seals (*A. tropicalis*) live on islands where cold Antarctic water meets warmer northern waters. Population: 300,000. **South African fur seals** (*A. pusillus pusillus*) and **Australian fur seals** (*A. pusillus doriferus*) are small groups within the species *Arctocephalus pusillus*. The first lives on the coasts of South Africa and Namibia. The second lives on the southern coast of Australia. Population: 1,200,000 South African seals; 25,000 Australian seals.

Northern Fur Seals

Scientific name: Callorhinus ursinus
*Length: females, 4.6 feet (1.4 m);
  males, 6.9 feet (2.1 m)*
*Weight: females, up to 110 pounds (50 kg);
  males, up to 595 pounds (270 kg)*

for mating purposes. They defend it against other bulls until the females arrive to give birth. The females nurse their young, but quickly lose interest in the mothering process. New matings take place only one week after the birth of pups from the previous mating season. One bull can mate with as many as one hundred females. During the two-month

All year long, there are more than one million northern fur seals together on the Pribilof islands.

The northern fur seal, sometimes referred to as the Pribilof or Alaska fur seal, lives over a wide area of the northern Pacific Ocean. Unfortunately, these are the seals most widely valued for the quality of their fur.

Although the northern fur seals migrate over large areas of water, reproduction takes place in only a few specific locations. Over 70 percent of all young are born on the Pribilof Islands near Alaska. First, males choose a territory each year by the beginning of June

mating period, the bulls do not eat at all. After mating, the harem breaks up, and the males go back to the sea. They stay there for the rest of the year. Mother seals will return to their pups but only about once a week for feeding. The pups usually gather together in groups until they are strong enough to swim out on their own.

Since these seals eat out at sea, it is difficult to observe their habits. Experts believe they eat mainly squid and fish.

Walruses

Scientific name: Odobenus rosmarus
Length: females, up to 8.5 feet (2.6 m);
males, up to 13 feet (4 m)
Weight: females, up to 2,756 pounds
(1250 kg); males, up to 3,528 pounds
(1600 kg)

The walrus's body looks somewhat like a wrinkled sausage. This animal has a small head with thick whiskers, through which large tusks hang down. The tusks are a sign of social rank. Bulls with the largest tusks have the highest rank, but they must work to earn their rank by fighting with other bulls.

The long, piercing tusks of the walrus have always been valued by humans. They serve a practical purpose for the walruses in their search for food on the ocean floor.

The walrus lives in the shallow waters of the coasts around the North Pole. The water there is about 330 feet (100 m) deep. The walrus prefers areas with a lot of moving ice, or ice floes. This way, it can rest on a solid surface and still be close to its food supply. Scientists estimate about 250,000 walruses live in the world today.

The whiskers also help the walrus find its food. It eats a variety of mussels and other soft animals that live on the ocean floor. The walrus glides along the floor with its head down, sucking in food almost like a vacuum cleaner. Its sensitive whiskers find mussels and snails. The walrus sucks out only the soft parts and leaves the shell.

Walruses have a rich eating place on the floor of the Bering Sea. Researchers have found that mollusks flourish there, and the walruses seem to cultivate their prey almost the way a farmer cultivates his or her crops.

Walruses are very social animals. Their pointed tusks never get in the way of others.

born between mid-April and mid-June.

Walrus calves have an easier time than most seal pups. Walruses are nursed for two to three years. Then, they make room for the next newborn calf. Killer whales and polar bears are natural enemies of the walruses and have been known to prey on them.

Scientists estimate that there are about 250,000 walruses in the world.

Grown bulls join a group of females during the mating season, which occurs in the winter season between January and April. Since mating and birth usually take place far out on ice floes, there is not very much specific information available about these processes. After mating, there is a four-month rest, then a gestation period of one year. Calves are

Humans have hunted the walrus for many years. Its ivory tusks are exquisitely suited for carving and were once considered more valuable than elephant tusks. Fortunately, the walrus is now protected by law. Inuits and other native people are the only ones allowed to hunt the walrus since they hunt the animal only for their daily living needs.

Protecting the Seals

Isn't this harp seal pup, with its trusting, innocent eyes, charming? It seems amazing that people could kill hundreds of thousands of these seals. But their fur was highly prized and used to make fur coats, so this practice went on for years without notice or comment. Then, the zoologist Bernhard Grzimek exposed the hunting practices. At first, hunters denied their role in the slaughter of seals. But before long, special laws protecting seals were passed. Since then, people's attitudes all over the world have changed. They have become more educated about seals and the problems associated with protecting them. Today, seals are no longer slaughtered. This terrible story had a happy ending. But the success in protecting seals should not stop with the seals. It should, rather, encourage people to work for the protection of all sea life and the irreplaceable waters that house them.

APPENDIX
TO
ANIMAL FAMILIES

SEALS

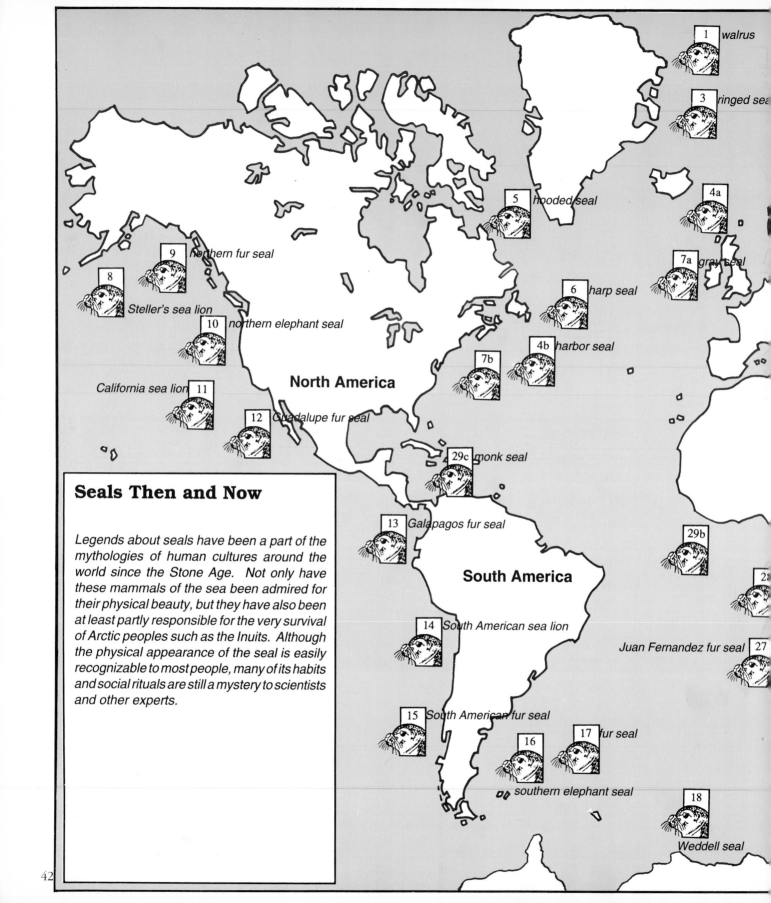

Seals Then and Now

Legends about seals have been a part of the mythologies of human cultures around the world since the Stone Age. Not only have these mammals of the sea been admired for their physical beauty, but they have also been at least partly responsible for the very survival of Arctic peoples such as the Inuits. Although the physical appearance of the seal is easily recognizable to most people, many of its habits and social rituals are still a mystery to scientists and other experts.

1 walrus
3 ringed seal
5 hooded seal
4a
7a gray seal
6 harp seal
9 northern fur seal
8 Steller's sea lion
10 northern elephant seal
4b harbor seal
7b
California sea lion 11
12 Guadalupe fur seal
29c monk seal
13 Galapagos fur seal
29b
North America
South America
14 South American sea lion
Juan Fernandez fur seal 27
15 South American fur seal
16
17 fur seal
18
southern elephant seal
Weddell seal

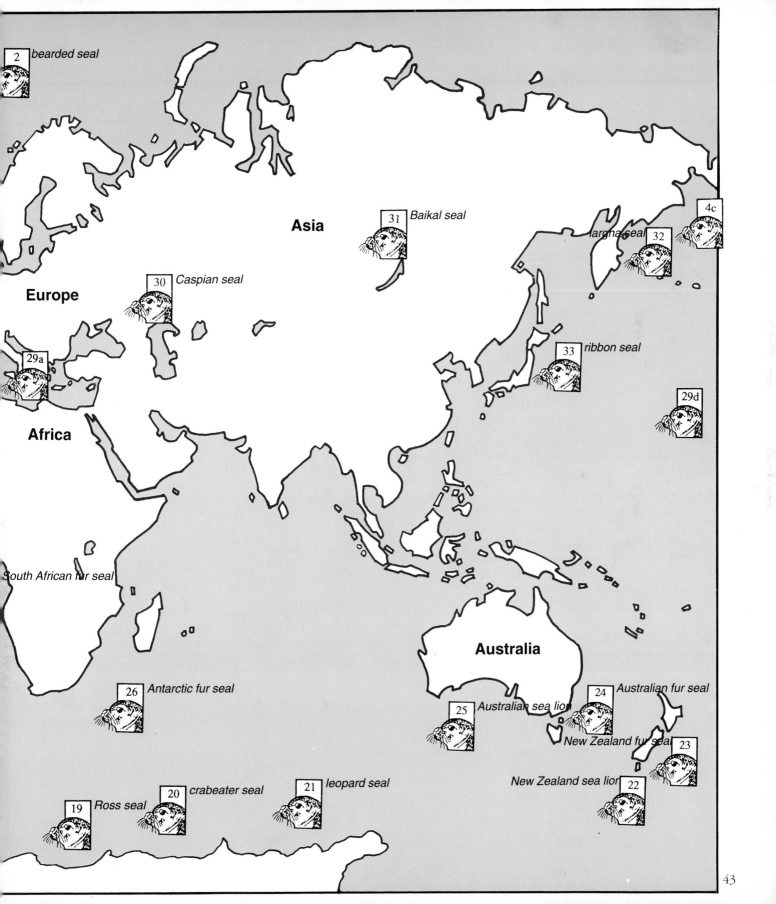

2 bearded seal

Asia

31 Baikal seal

4c

largha seal

32

Europe

30 Caspian seal

33 ribbon seal

29a

29d

Africa

South African fur seal

Australia

26 Antarctic fur seal

24 Australian fur seal

25 Australian sea lion

New Zealand fur seal

23

New Zealand sea lion

22

19 Ross seal

20 crabeater seal

21 leopard seal

ABOUT THESE BOOKS

Although this series is called "Animal Families," these books aren't just about fathers, mothers, and young. They also discuss the scientific definition of *family,* which is a division of biological classification and includes many animals.

Biological classification is a method that scientists use to identify and organize living things. Using this system, scientists place animals and plants into larger groups that share similar characteristics. Characteristics are physical features, natural habits, ancestral backgrounds, or any other qualities that make one organism either like or different from another.

The method used today for biological classification was introduced in 1753 by a Swedish botanist-naturalist named Carolus Linnaeus. Although many scientists tried to find ways to classify the world's plants and animals, Linnaeus's system seemed to be the only useful choice. Charles Darwin, a famous British naturalist, referred to Linnaeus's system in his theory of evolution, which was published in his book *On the Origin of Species* in 1859. Linnaeus's system of classification, shown below, includes seven major categories, or groups. These are: kingdom, phylum, class, order, family, genus, and species.

An easy way to remember the divisions and their order is to memorize this sentence: "Ken Put Cake On Frank's Good Shirt." The first letter of each word in this sentence gives you the first letter of a division. (The *K* in *Ken*, for example, stands for *kingdom*.) The order of the words in this sentence suggests the order of the divisions from largest to smallest. The kingdom is the largest of these divisions; the species is the smallest. The larger the division, the more types of animals or plants it contains. For example, the animal kingdom, called Animalia, contains everything from worms to whales. Smaller divisions, such as the family, have fewer members that share more characteristics. For example, members of the bear family, Ursidae, include the polar bear, the brown bear, and many others.

In the following chart, the lion species is followed through all seven categories. As the categories expand to include more and more members, remember that only a few examples are pictured here. Each division has many more members.

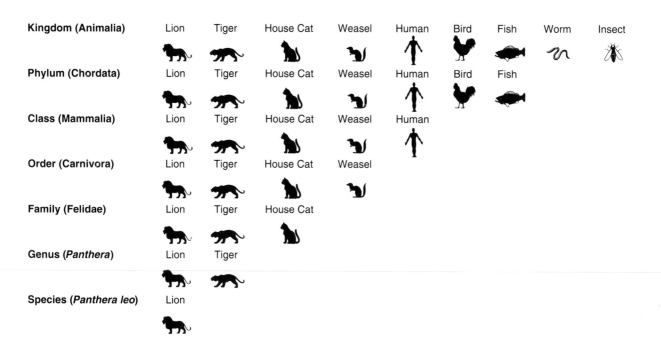

Kingdom (Animalia)	Lion	Tiger	House Cat	Weasel	Human	Bird	Fish	Worm	Insect
Phylum (Chordata)	Lion	Tiger	House Cat	Weasel	Human	Bird	Fish		
Class (Mammalia)	Lion	Tiger	House Cat	Weasel	Human				
Order (Carnivora)	Lion	Tiger	House Cat	Weasel					
Family (Felidae)	Lion	Tiger	House Cat						
Genus (*Panthera*)	Lion	Tiger							
Species (*Panthera leo*)	Lion								

SCIENTIFIC NAMES OF THE ANIMALS IN THIS BOOK

Animals have different names in every language. For this reason, researchers the world over use the same scientific names, which usually stem from ancient Greek or Latin. Most animals are classified by two names. One is the genus name; the other is the name of the species to which they belong. Additional names indicate further subgroupings. Here is a list of the animals included in *Seals.*

Harbor seal	*Phoca vitulina*
Largha seal	*Phoca largha*
Ringed seal	*Phoca hispida*
Caspian seal	*Phoca caspica*
Baikal seal	*Phoca sibirica*
Harp seal	*Phoca groenlandica*
Ribbon seal	*Phoca fasciata*
Gray seal	*Halichoerus grypus*
Hooded seal	*Cystophora cristata*
Bearded seal	*Erignathus barbatus*
Mediterranean monk seal	*Monachus monachus*
Weddell seal	*Leptonychotes weddelli*
Crabeater seal	*Lobodon carcinophagus*

Leopard seal	*Hydrurga leptonyx*
Ross seal	*Ommatophoca rossi*
Southern elephant seal	*Mirounga leonina*
Northern elephant seal	*Mirounga angustirostris*
California sea lion	*Zalophus californianus*
Steller's sea lion	*Eumetopias jubatus*
Southern sea lion	*Otaria byronia*
Australian sea lion	*Neophoca cinerea*
New Zealand sea lion	*Phocarctos hookeri*
Southern fur seals	*Arctocephalus pusillus*
Northern fur seal	*Callorhinus ursinus*
Walrus	*Odobenus rosmarus*

GLOSSARY

activists
People who take strong, direct action in support of or against a cause.

amplifier
A device that increases the volume of sound, thereby making a sound easier to hear.

ancestors
Persons from whom one is descended; a forerunner or predecessor.

class
The third of seven divisions in the biological classification system proposed by Swedish botanist-naturalist Carolus Linnaeus. The class is the main subdivision of the phylum. Seals belong to the class Mammalia. Animals in this class, which includes humans, share certain features: they have skin covered with hair, they give birth to live young, and they nourish the young with milk from mammary glands.

colonies
Members of the same species who gather together in a group.

endangered animals
Animals that have become rare and are threatened with extinction, usually because of human behavior or a change in environmental conditions.

epidemic
An outbreak of disease that spreads rapidly and widely.

extinction
The end or destruction of a specific type of living organism (plant or animal).

family
The fifth of seven divisions in the biological classification system proposed by Swedish botanist-naturalist Carolus Linnaeus. Seals belong to the family Phocidae.

fertile
Productive, or capable of reproducing.

flipper
A wide, flat limb of an animal that is used for swimming.

floe
A large sheet of ice that floats on the top of the water.

follicle
A small hole or deep, narrow depression.

genus (plural: **genera**)
The sixth division in the biological classification system proposed by Swedish botanist-naturalist Carolus Linnaeus. A genus is the main subdivision of a family and includes one or more species.

germination
The developing or sprouting of an organism.

gestation period
The number of days from actual conception to the birth of an animal. Gestation periods vary greatly for different types of animals.

gout
A disease that causes painful inflammation and swelling of the joints.

grotto
A cave.

harem
A group of females associated with only one male.

hereditary
Having a feature or characteristic that is passed on from one generation to the next.

instinct
A natural action that is undertaken without involving the thought process.

kingdom
The first of seven divisions in the biological classification system proposed by Swedish botanist-naturalist Carolus Linnaeus. Animals, including humans, belong to the kingdom Animalia. It is one of five kingdoms.

krill
Small, shrimplike creatures that live in the open sea. Krill form an important part of the animal food chain and are eaten by fish, seals, birds, and whales.

mate (verb)
To join together (animals) to produce offspring.

molt
To shed or change fur, skin, hair, feathers, or any outer layer from time to time. The molting season for harbor seals, for example, is in late summer.

nimble
Having or possessing quick and light movements. Seals are very nimble animals in the water even though they are quite awkward on land.

order
The fourth of seven divisions in the biological classification system proposed by the Swedish botanist-naturalist Carolus Linnaeus. The order is the main subdivision of the class and contains many different families. Seals belong to the order Pinnipedia.

phylum (plural: **phyla**)
The second of seven divisions in the biological classification system proposed by the Swedish botanist-naturalist Carolus Linnaeus. A phylum is one of the main divisions of a kingdom.

predator
An animal that lives by eating other animals.

prey
Any creature that is hunted or caught as food.

propagating
Increasing in number through reproduction.

solitary
Living or wanting to live alone; not social

species
The last of seven divisions in the biological classification system proposed by Swedish botanist-naturalist Carolus Linnaeus. The species is the main subdivision of the genus. It may include further subgroups of its own, called subspecies. At the level of species, members share many features and are capable of breeding with one another.

virus
A submicroscopic parasite that can multiply within cells and cause disease.

MORE BOOKS ABOUT SEALS

Creatures of the Sea. Science Adventures (Price Stern)
Elephant Seals. Sylvia Johnson (Lerner)
The Sea World Book of Seals and Sea Lions. Phyllis R. Evans (Harcourt Brace Jovanovich)
The Seal on the Rocks. Doug Allan (Gareth Stevens)
Seals and Sea Lions. Wildlife Education, Ltd., Staff (Wildlife Education)
Seals of the World. Judith E. King (Cornell University)
Seasons of the Seal. Fred Bruemmer (Northword)
Wavebender: A Story of Daniel au Fond. Tom Shachtman (Henry Holt)

PLACES TO WRITE

The following are some of the many organizations that exist to educate people about animals, promote the protection of animals, and encourage the conservation of their environments. Write to these organizations for more information about seals, other animals, or animal concerns of interest to you. When you write, include your name, address, and age, and tell them clearly what you want to know. Don't forget to enclose a stamped, self-addressed envelope for a reply.

Animal Protection Institute
P.O. Box 22505
Sacramento, CA 95822

California Marine Mammal Center
Marin Headlands Ranger Station
Fort Cronkite, CA 94965

The Cousteau Society
425 East 52nd Street
New York, NY 10022

Marine Science Research Center
State University of New York
Stony Brook, NY 11790

Oceanic Society
Fort Mason Center
Building E
San Francisco, CA 94123

World Wildlife Fund (Canada)
90 Eglinton Avenue East, Suite 504
Toronto, Ontario M4P 2Z7

THINGS TO DO

These projects are designed to help you have fun with what you've learned about seals. You can do them alone, in small groups, or as a class project.

1. Plan a visit to the marine area of the nearest zoo. What types of seals did you see there? Were there several types of seals or many seals of the same species?

2. Make a chart that includes information about the various seals. This will help you see how their features are alike and how they are different.

3. Look at a world map or a globe and identify the areas that seals inhabit.

4. Watch your television listings for programs that feature sea animals, especially seals.

5. Draw a picture of your favorite seal. Why is it your favorite?

INDEX